The *Heroic* Symphony

Anna Harwell Celenza

Illustrated by
JoAnn E. Kitchel

Charlesbridge

Published by Charlesbridge
85 Main Street, Watertown, MA 02472
(617) 926-0329
www.charlesbridge.com

Library of Congress Cataloging-in-Publication Data
Celenza, Anna Harwell.
The heroic symphony/Anna Harwell Celenza; illustrated by JoAnn E. Kitchel.
p.   cm.
Summary: After learning that he is going deaf, Beethoven is determined
to write a great symphony and thinks he has found his inspiration
in the heroic deeds of Napoleon.
ISBN 1-57091-509-1 (reinforced for library use)
1. Beethoven, Ludwig van, 1770-1827—Juvenile fiction. [1. Beethoven,
Ludwig van, 1770-1827—Fiction. 2. Composers—Fiction.]
I. Kitchel, JoAnn E., ill. II. Title.
PZ7.C314 He   2004
[E]—dc21   2003003732

Manufactured in Singapore
(hc) 10 9 8 7 6 5 4 3 2 1

Illustrations done in watercolor and ink on Arches cold press paper
Display type and text type set in Giovanni and Della Robbia
Color separations, printing, and binding by Imago
Production supervision by Brian G. Walker
Designed by Diane M. Earley

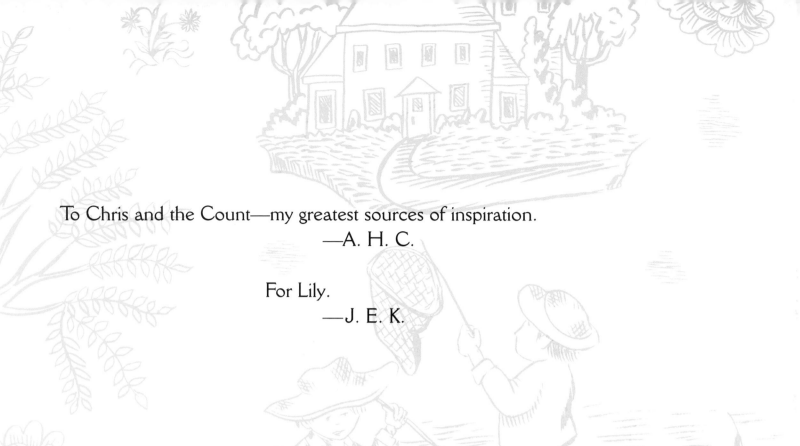

To Chris and the Count—my greatest sources of inspiration.
—A. H. C.

For Lily.
—J. E. K.

A Note About the CD Recording:
Tracks 1–4 are the four movements of Beethoven's *Heroic* Symphony.
Track 5 is a bonus selection of "Overture to Goethe's tragedy *Egmont*."

n a glimmering salon, Ludwig van Beethoven played the piano. The audience sat mesmerized. Never had they heard music performed with such emotion and strength. As Ludwig glanced at them, he felt extremely proud. He was the best pianist in Vienna, perhaps the best in all of Europe. Ludwig wrote music that showcased his talent, and when he played, women swooned and men cheered. The wealthy paid him large sums of money to perform in their homes.

It seemed he had everything: talent, fame, money. No one suspected that the great Ludwig van Beethoven also had a troubling secret—he was slowly going deaf. It was getting more and more difficult for him to play the piano. Without his hearing his career, fame, and fortune would soon come to an end.

Ludwig searched in secret for a treatment that would restore his hearing, but without success. Then a doctor in Heiligenstadt promised he could help. Filled with hope, Ludwig left Vienna in the spring of 1802 to stay at the remote clinic.

In Heiligenstadt, Ludwig did everything the doctor recommended. He ate a special diet, exercised regularly, and rested his ears by staying away from concerts and avoiding long conversations. As the months passed, however, his hearing only grew worse. Finally, in October, the doctor delivered the dreaded news—the treatment was a failure. Ludwig was going deaf, and his career as a pianist was over.

"No!" cried Ludwig. "It can't be true!" Anger welled up inside him. He stood up without saying another word and ran out the door.

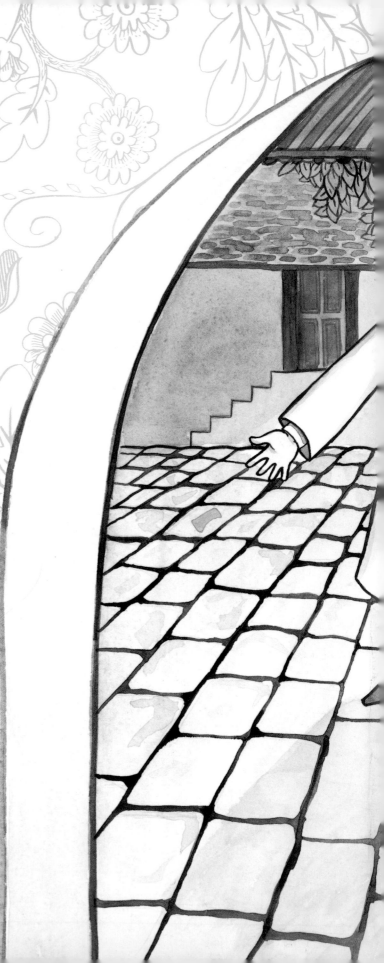

Ludwig walked for hours, through the woods, along the river. He tried to make sense of the horrible news, but the same thought kept running through his mind: "Without performing, without my music, what reason is there to live?" Sorrow and fear crept into his heart.

In his room Ludwig began writing a farewell letter to his brothers. He tried to explain the horror of his situation, but finding the right words was difficult. As he sat at his desk, a sorrowful melody filled his imagination. Ludwig listened to the tune— it expressed his thoughts and emotions in a way words could not. And while he listened, something happened: Ludwig's will to live grew stronger.

"My ears might be failing, but music has not abandoned me," he thought. "If I can imagine music—then I can write it! I will be a composer—as great a composer as I was a pianist!" Filled with renewed hope, Ludwig packed his bags and returned to Vienna.

Ludwig visited all his old friends. He had left the city without saying good-bye, and many wondered where he had been. Now, one by one, each learned of Ludwig's tragic fate. Some were indifferent to the news. Others treated him as an invalid. Ludwig soon learned who his real friends were. Ferdinand, a fellow musician, was one of them.

"Becoming a great composer is what gives my life meaning," Ludwig explained to Ferdinand. "I won't write music that just entertains people. I will write music that exhilarates them! I want people to think when they hear my music! I want to touch their souls! But I must find inspiration. Something great, someone heroic."

Over the next few months, Ludwig searched diligently for inspiration. He read the newspapers and talked with friends. It soon became clear that one figure towered above the rest—a war hero named Napoleon Bonaparte. In just a few years, Bonaparte had rid France of an unjust king, created a government run by the people, and promised religious freedom and education to all. "He has carved out his own destiny and accomplished the impossible," thought Ludwig as he read the paper one morning. "He deserves a musical tribute."

Ludwig went to his piano. He thought about Bonaparte's great deeds and tried to compose, but no melodies came to him. Frustrated, he pocketed a small notebook and went for a walk.

Ludwig's hearing had not yet failed completely. As he walked through the park, he struggled to follow the conversations of those around him. Everyone was praising Bonaparte. Young women pushing baby carriages swooned over his good looks and chivalry. Two men playing checkers praised his bravery and political talent. Even the old man at the newsstand sang his praises: "Bonaparte is a man of the people, a bringer of peace. The kings of England and Prussia are afraid. They have declared war against Bonaparte. But I'm not afraid."

"Nor I!" said a young boy. He grabbed a magazine with Bonaparte's picture on it and handed it to Ludwig. "Just wait and see," said the boy. "One day Bonaparte will save us all!"

Ludwig studied the cover of the magazine carefully. Napoleon Bonaparte charged forward on a magnificent stallion, afraid of nothing, certain of victory. Ludwig thought about his own struggles, his battle with deafness, and his courage to carry on. Suddenly a bold, heroic melody came to him. "That's it!" he cried. He opened his notebook and jotted down the tune. Then he raced home. He rushed to the piano without taking off his hat and stormed on for hours—writing, playing, rewriting—with ideas for a new symphony.

Ludwig worked on the symphony for five long months, blending his own life story and his hopes as a composer into the heroic tale of Bonaparte. One after another the four movements took their form. Ferdinand visited regularly, and on each occasion Ludwig shared passages of the symphony and explained his inspiration.

"I call it the *Bonaparte* Symphony," said Ludwig. "It is a reflection of his courage and heroic character, his struggle against fate. The first movement is a battle scene. Shield against shield and helmet to helmet, Bonaparte fights the injustice that plagues us all."

Ferdinand looked at the score. He could almost hear the music in his mind. Ludwig had transformed the timpani into cannon blasts, the horns into battle calls. The woodwinds sang a song of lament while the strings galloped forward across wind-swept fields.

The hairs stood up on the back of Ferdinand's neck. "This is no earthly battle," he thought. Indeed Ludwig's own fears and struggles, his battle against deafness, and his fight against fate, had gone into the making of the music.

A few weeks later, Ludwig showed Ferdinand the second movement. He had been thinking of a funeral procession when he wrote this section, and it was filled with a sense of longing and anxiety. Ferdinand could hear the steady footsteps of mourners passing by. Ludwig played a section of the movement on the piano. "I was imagining Bonaparte on the battlefield when I began to write this part," he said. "But it evolved into something more—my own suffering . . . the sorrows of humanity."

A haunting sorrow filled Ferdinand's heart. He could almost feel the specter of death around him. Ferdinand was shaken when he left Ludwig's apartment.

On another visit Ludwig showed Ferdinand the third movement, a dance of celebration. "The battle is over," said Ludwig. "Fear and death have been conquered. Hope appears on the horizon, warm and bright—a joyous homecoming!"

Ferdinand studied the music carefully. In the distance he could hear a lilting melody rise up from the strings. Slowly it grew louder. Then, like a sunbeam, it filled the room with light. Ferdinand's heart beat faster as horn calls responded to the happy tune. "This is pure pleasure!" he cried.

"The indescribable joy of being alive!" shouted Ludwig, banging out a few chords on the piano.

The fourth movement was the most difficult to write. Ludwig struggled with it for weeks. The legend of Prometheus served as inspiration. The way Ludwig saw it, Prometheus had brought mankind comfort with the gift of fire, and Bonaparte would soon bring peace with the gift of liberty.

Ferdinand studied the final pages of the symphony. A tranquil melody appeared over and over, changing slightly every time. He heard the full range of human emotions—love, anger, sorrow, joy. A sense of peace and comfort swept over him. Ferdinand's soul was transformed, elevated to a higher realm.

He listened to the music and realized that it was not the genius of Bonaparte he heard, but the blessing of a musical genius. "Ludwig, you did it!" he cried. "You've created a true masterpiece!"

Over the next couple of weeks, Ludwig put the final touches on his symphony. He made a second copy to send to Napoleon Bonaparte as a gift. He was putting the copy in an envelope when he heard loud shouts from the street below. Ludwig looked out the window and caught sight of Ferdinand.

"What's going on?" he called.

"Oh, tragedy!" cried Ferdinand. "All is lost!"

"What are you talking about?" shouted Ludwig.

Ferdinand held up a newspaper. "Bonaparte betrayed us all!" he cried. "He has crowned himself Emperor of France!"

Ludwig's face grew red with anger. "So he, too, is nothing but a greedy man who puts himself above the rest of us!"

Ludwig rushed to the piano, grabbed his new symphony, and began ripping it to shreds. As the final pieces fell to the floor, Ferdinand burst through the door. "What have you done?" he cried.

"I did not write my symphony for a tyrant!" shouted Ludwig.

Ferdinand saw the extra copy on the desk and grabbed it.

"Give that to me!" roared Ludwig.

Ferdinand shook his head. "I won't let you destroy it!" he cried, and held the music tighter.

Despair swept over Ludwig. He looked down at the scraps of paper scattered around his feet. He thought of the many months he had worked on his symphony—all the hopes and dreams that had gone into the music. Melodies from the symphony played through his mind, reminding him of his own struggle with fate.

Slowly his anger subsided. Ludwig went to his friend and said, "Please, Ferdinand, give me my music. I promise not to destroy it."

Ferdinand laid the music on the table.

"This symphony isn't about Bonaparte," said Ludwig. "It never was. It's about me, and you—about humanity—the hero in each and every one of us." Ludwig took a quill from the inkstand and scratched out the word "Bonaparte" until a hole appeared in the paper. Then, in large letters, he wrote a new title across the page:

The Heroic Symphony

When the *Heroic* Symphony was first performed in 1804, no one in the audience knew the story behind the work—that was a secret between Ludwig and Ferdinand. Everyone who heard the music was moved by its majesty. In the splendor of each movement, listeners discovered their own hopes and fears—their own struggles against fate. As a composer Ludwig van Beethoven made audiences think. The *Heroic* Symphony touched their souls.

Author's Note

The Heroic Symphony tells the true story behind the creation of Beethoven's Symphony No. 3, commonly known as the *Eroica* Symphony (Italian for "heroic"). The events in this story and its central characters are all drawn from 19th-century sources.

When Beethoven first arrived in Vienna in 1792, he was best known for his skills as a performer. As a peer explained, "His playing dashed along at full tilt like a waterfall frothing wildly." Letters written by Beethoven indicate that his hearing difficulties began in the mid-1790s. When the doctor in Heiligenstadt told him that his deafness was incurable, he wrote his brothers a letter now known as "The Heiligenstadt Testament." This is one of the most fascinating documents in music history. Written over a period of several days (October 6-10, 1802), the letter reflects Beethoven's inner thoughts, including his brief contemplation of suicide and eventual decision to carry on as a composer.

My descriptions of the *Heroic* Symphony's four movements are drawn from reviews published shortly after its premiere. As inspiration for the fourth movement, Beethoven reused a melody he wrote for a ballet about Prometheus. According to Beethoven the melody represented "a sublime spirit who came upon the people of his time and refined them through science and art."

The connection between Napoleon Bonaparte and the *Heroic* Symphony was not common knowledge during Beethoven's lifetime. In fact Napoleon's influence was not made public until 1838 (11 years after Beethoven's death), when Ferdinand Ries published a biographical study of the composer:

> *"I was the first to tell [Beethoven] the news that Bonaparte had crowned himself emperor, whereupon he shouted: 'So he too is nothing more than an ordinary man. Now he will trample all human rights underfoot and only pander to his own ambition; he will place himself above everyone else and become a tyrant!'"* Beethoven reportedly then took the score, *"ripped it all the way through, and flung it to the floor. The title page was written again, and only then did the symphony receive the title* Sinfonia eroica.*"*

Unfortunately Beethoven's original manuscript of the symphony no longer exists. But a copy of it with corrections made in Beethoven's hand can be found at the Gesellschaft der Musikfreunde in Vienna. This copy bears the revised title page described in this book.

The *Heroic* Symphony was not Beethoven's only Napoleon-inspired composition. In 1813 he celebrated Napoleon's defeat at the Battle of Waterloo with a symphonic work entitled *Wellington's Victory.*